QUICK LANGUAGES

MULTI-LANGUAGE PHRASEBOOK COLLECTION

ENGLISH-PORTUGUESE
PORTUGUESE-ENGLISH

QUICK LANGUAGES

MULTI-LANGUAGE PHRASEBOOK COLLECTION

SPEAK ANY LANGUAGE NOW!

WHAT IS QUICK LANGUAGES?

Did you know that we only use about 1,000 words in our everyday vocabulary? The same goes for any language! So, mastering a digital phrasebook with interactive pronunciation tools is a smart alternative to long and expensive language instruction.

Quick Languages is an interactive phrasebook that introduces you to the 12 predominant world languages all in one convenient drop-down menu. Designed for visual, auditory, and kinesthetic learners alike, it is simple, affordable, and effective.

Own the potential of connecting with over 3 billion people!

QUICK LANGUAGES

MULTI-LANGUAGE PHRASEBOOK COLLECTION

SPEAK ANY LANGUAGE NOW!

QUICK LANGUAGES PHRASEBOOK COLLECTION AVAILABLE TITLES

1. ENGLISH-SPANISH & SPANISH-ENGLISH
2. ENGLISH-ITALIAN & ITALIAN-ENGLISH
3. ENGLISH-FRENCH & FRENCH-ENGLISH
4. ENGLISH-GERMAN & GERMAN-ENGLISH
5. ENGLISH-PORTUGUESE & PORTUGUESE-ENGLISH
6. ENGLISH-CHINESE & CHINESE-ENGLISH
7. ENGLISH-ARABIC & ARABIC-ENGLISH
8. ENGLISH-JAPANESE & JAPANESE-ENGLISH
9. ENGLISH-KOREAN & KOREAN-ENGLISH
10. ENGLISH-RUSSIAN & RUSSIAN-ENGLISH
11. ENGLISH-TURKISH & TURKISH-ENGLISH

COMPANION ONLINE COURSE
quicklanguages.com

Quick Languages: 1,000 Key Words and Expressions Phrasebook
ENGLISH-PORTUGUESE & PORTUGUESE-ENGLISH

Paperback ISBN: 978-1-681656-11-3

Library of Congress Control Code: 2023932218

First paperback edition: April 2023

Edited by Gregorio García
Cover art by Natalia Urbano
Layout by Esmeralda Riveros & Pancho Guijarro

Printed in the USA

American Book Group
americanbookgroup.com

INDEX OF CONTENTS

1,000 KEY WORDS AND EXPRESSIONS

English / Portuguese - Portuguese / English

Keep practicing at:
QuickLanguages.com

1. Greetings / Cumprimentos

English	Portuguese
Hi! / Hello!	**Olá!**
Good morning	**Bom dia**
Good afternoon	**Boa tarde**
Good evening / Good night	**Boa noite**
How are you doing?	**Como está você?**
Fine	**Bem**
Very well	**Muito bem**
Thank you / Thanks	**Obrigado(a)**
Thank you very much	**Muito obrigado(a)**
You're welcome	**De nada**
Fine, thank you	**Bem, obrigado(a)**
And you?	**E você?**
See you	**A gente se vê**
See you later	**Até logo**
See you tomorrow	**Até amanhã**
Goodbye	**Adeus**
Bye	**Tchau**

2. Introductions and Courtesy Expressions / **Apresentações e Expressões de Cortesia**

What is your name?	**Qual o seu nome?**
My name is ...	**Meu nome é...**
Who are you?	**Quem é você?**
I am ...	**Sou...**
Who is he / she?	**Quem é ele/ela?**
He is ... / She is ...	**Ele é.../Ela é...**
Nice to meet you / Pleased to meet you	**Prazer em conhecê-lo/la**
Nice to meet you, too	**Prazer em conhecê-lo/la também**
It's my pleasure	**É um prazer**
Excuse me	**Desculpe**
Please	**Por favor**
One moment, please	**Um momento, por favor**
Welcome	**Bem-vindo**
Go ahead	**Você primeiro**
Can you repeat, please?	**Pode repetir, por favor?**
I don't understand	**Não compreendo**
I understand a little	**Compreendo um pouco**
Can you speak more slowly, please?	**Você poderia falar mais devagar, por favor?**
Do you speak Spanish?	**Você fala espanhol?**
How do you say hello in Spanish?	**Como se diz hello em espanhol?**
What does it mean?	**O que significa isso?**
I speak Spanish a little	**Falo um pouco de espanhol**

3. Ways to Address to a Person / **Maneiras de se Dirigir a uma Pessoa**

Madam / Ma'am	**Senhora**
Miss	**Senhorita**
Ms.	**Sra.,Srta.**
Mr.	**Senhor**
Mrs.	**Senhora**
Sir	**Senhor**
Dr.	**Doutor**

4. The Articles / **Os Artigos**

The	**O / a / os / as**
The car	**O automóvel**
The cars	**Os automóveis**
The house	**A casa**
The houses	**As casas**
A	**Um / uma**
A car	**Um automóvel**
A house	**Uma casa**
An	**Um / uma**
An elephant	**Um elefante**
An apple	**Uma maçã**
Some	**Uns / umas**
Some cars	**Uns automóveis**
Some houses	**Umas casas**

5. The Subject Pronouns / Os Pronomes Pessoais de Sujeito

I	**Eu**
You	**Tu / Você (Vc)**
He	**Ele**
She	**Ela**
It	**Isso**
We	**Nós**
You	**Vocês**
They	**Eles / elas**

6. The Possessive Adjectives / Os Adjetivos Possessivos

My	**Mim**
Your	**Tu**
His	**Seu (dele)**
Her	**Sua (dela)**
Its	**Seu**
Our	**Nosso/a**
Your	**De vocês /Vosso (a)**
Their	**Seus (deles/delas)**
My car	**Meu carro**
Your book	**Teu livro**
His TV	**Sua televisão**
Our house	**Nossa casa**

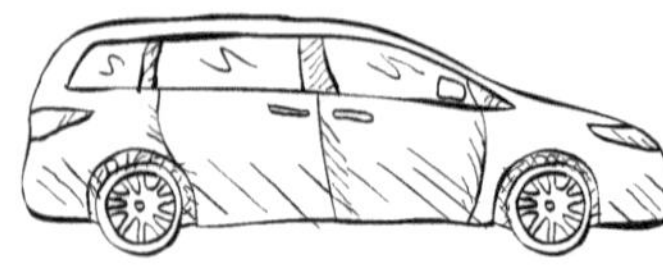

7. The Demonstrative Adjectives **/ Os Adjetivos Demonstrativos**

This	**Este / esta**
This book	**Este livro**
This shirt	**Esta camisa**
These	**Estes / estas**
These books	**Estes livros**
These shirts	**Estas camisas**
That	**Esse / essa**
That table	**Essa mesa**
That car	**Esse carro**
Those	**Esses / essas**
Those tables	**Essas mesas**
Those cars	**Esses carros**

8. The Possessive Pronouns **/ Os Pronomes Possessivos**

Mine	**Meu**
Yours	**Teu**
His	**Seu (dele)**
Hers	**sua (dela)**
Its	**Seu**
Ours	**Nosso/a**
Yours	**Vosso**
Theirs	**Seu (deles / delas)**
The car is mine	**O carro é meu**
The book is yours	**O livro é teu**
That TV is his	**Essa tevisão é sua**
This house is ours	**Esta casa é nossa**

9. The Cardinal Numbers / Os Numerais Cardinais

0 / Zero	**Zero**
1 / One	**Um**
2 / Two	**Dois**
3 / Three	**Três**
4 / Four	**Quatro**
5 / Five	**Cinco**
6 / Six	**Seis**
7 / Seven	**Sete**
8 / Eight	**Oito**
9 / Nine	**Nove**
10 / Ten	**Dez**
11 / Eleven	**Onze**
12 / Twelve	**Doze**
13 / Thirteen	**Treze**
14 / Fourteen	**Catorze**
15 / Fifteen	**Quinze**
16 / Sixteen	**Dezesseis**
17 / Seventeen	**Dezessete**
18 / Eighteen	**dezoito**
19 / Nineteen	**dezenove**
20 / Twenty	**Vinte**
21 / Twenty-one	**Vinte e um**
30 / Thirty	**Trinta**
40 / Forty	**Quarenta**
50 / Fifty	**Cinquenta**
60 / Sixty	**Sessenta**

9. The Cardinal Numbers / Os Numerais Cardinais

70 / Seventy	**Setenta**
80 / Eighty	**Oitenta**
90 /Ninety	**Noventa**
100 / One hundred	**Cem**
101 / One hundred and one	**Cento e um**
200 / Two hundred	**Duzentos**
300 / Three hundred	**Trezentos**
400 / Four hundred	**Quatrocentos**
500 / Five hundred	**Quinhentos**
600 / Six hundred	**Seiscentos**
700 / Seven hundred	**Setecentos**
800 / Eight hundred	**Oitocentos**
900 /Nine hundred	**Novecentos**
1,000 / One thousand	**Mil**
10,000 / Ten thousand	**Dez mil**
100,000 / One hundred thousand	**Cem mil**
1,000,000 / One million	**Um milhão**
1,000,000,000 / One billion	**Mil milhões**
Forty-five (45)	**Quarente e cinco**
One hundred and twenty-eight (128)	**Cento e vinte e oito**
One thousand nine hundred and sixty-three (1,963)	**Mil novecentos e sessenta e três**
Six thousand and thirty-seven (6,037)	**Seis mil e trinta e sete**
Eleven thousand (11,000)	**Onze mil**
Two hundred and seventy-nine thousand (279,000)	**Duzentos e setenta e nove mil**
Two million (2,000,000)	**Dois milhões**

10. The Time / A Hora

The clock	**O relógio (de pared)**
The watch	**O relógio (de pulso)**
What time is it?	**Que horas são?**
It is ...	**São...**
It is one o'clock (1:00)	**É uma hora**
It is two o'clock (2:00)	**São duas horas**
It is three fifteen / It is a quarter past three (3:15)	**São três e quinze**
It is four thirty / It is half past four (4:30)	**São quatro e trinta / São as quatro e meia**
It is five forty-five / It is a quarter to six (5:45)	**São cinco e quarenta e cinco / São quinze para as seis**
It is six fifty / It is ten to seven (6:50)	**São seis e cinquenta / São dez para as sete**
It is noon (12:00 P. M.)	**É meio-dia**
It is midnight (12:00 A. M.)	**É meia-noite**
In the morning	**Na manhã**
In the afternoon	**Na tarde**
In the evening	**Na noite**
At night	**Na noite**
At what time is ...?	**Que hora é....?**
At what time is the concert?	**Que hora é o show?**
At ...	**à / às**
At 7:10 P.M. (seven ten in the evening)	**Às sete da noite**

11. The Days of the Week / **Os Dias da Semana**

English	Portuguese
Monday	**Segunda-feira**
Tuesday	**Terça-feira**
Wednesday	**Quarta-feira**
Thursday	**Quinta-feira**
Friday	**Sexta-feira**
Saturday	**Sábado**
Sunday	**Domingo**
What day is today?	**Que dia é hoje?**

12. The Months of the Year / **Os Meses do Ano**

English	Portuguese
January	**Janeiro**
February	**Fevereiro**
March	**Março**
April	**Abril**
May	**Maio**
June	**Junho**
July	**Julho**
August	**Agosto**
September	**Setembro**
October	**Outubro**
November	**Novembro**
December	**Dezembro**
What is today's date?	**Qual a data de hoje?**

13. The Weather **/ O Clima**

Sunny	**Ensolarado**
Cloudy	**Nublado**
Rainy	**Chuvoso**
Humid	**Húmido**
Dry	**Seco**
Cold	**Frio**
Warm	**Calor**
Hot	**Calor**
Rain	**A chuva**
Snow	**A neve**
How is the weather today?	**Como está o clima hoje?**
It's nice	**O clima está bom**
It's sunny	**Está soleado**
It's cold in winter	**Faz frio no inverno**
It's raining	**Está chovendo**
It's snowing	**Está nevando**
I am cold	**Tenho frio**

14. The Seasons / As Estações

Spring	**Primavera**
Summer	**Verão**
Fall	**Outono**
Winter	**Inverno**

15. The Colors / As Cores

Yellow	**Amarelo**
Red	**Vermelho**
Blue	**Azul**
Green	**Verde**
Orange	**Laranja**
Brown	**Marrom**
Pink	**Cor-de rosa**
Purple	**Púrpura**
Black	**Preto**
White	**Branco**
Gray	**Cinza**
Light	**Claro**
Dark	**Escuro**
Light green	**Verde-claro**
Orange book	**Livro laranja**
Brown shoes	**Sapatos marrons**
My blouse is white	**Minha blusa é branca**
What color is...?	**De que cor é...?**
What is your favorite color?	**Qual a tua cor favorita?**

16. The Parts of the Face / As Partes da Casa

Cheek	**A bochecha**
Chin	**O queixo**
Ear	**A orelha**
Eye	**O olho**
Forehead	**A testa**
Hair	**O cabelo**
Lips	**Os lábios**
Mouth	**A boca**
Nose	**O nariz**
Skin	**A pele**
Teeth	**Os dentes**
Tooth	**O dente**
Blond / Blonde	**Louro / Loura**
Brown	**Castanho**
Gray	**Com cabelo branco**
Red hair	**Ruivo**
Long	**Comprido**
Short	**Curto**
Straight	**Liso**
Curly	**Enrrolado**
John is blond	**John é louro**
Karen has long hair	**Karen tem cabelo comprido**
He has green eyes	**Ele tem olhos verdes**
Her eyes are blue	**Seus olhos são azuis**
His eyes are big and brown	**Seus olhos são grandes e marrons**

17. Essential Verbs / Verbos Essenciais

Be	**Ser / Estar**
Go	**Ir**
Come	**Vir**
Have	**Ter**
Get	**Conseguir**
Help	**Ajudar**
Love	**Amar**
Like	**Gostar**
Want	**Querer**
Buy	**Comprar**
Sell	**Vender**
Read	**Ler**
Write	**Escrever**
Drink	**Beber**
Eat	**Comer**
Open	**Abrir**
Close	**Fechar**
Look at	**Olhar**
Look for	**Buscar**
Find	**Encontrar**
Start	**Começar**
Stop	**Parar**
Pull	**Puxar**

17. Essential Verbs / Verbos Essenciais

Push	**Empurrar**
Send	**Enviar**
Receive	**Receber**
Turn on	**Acender**
Turn off	**Apagar**
Listen to	**Escutar**
Speak	**Falar**
Do	**Fazer**
Drive	**Dirigir**
Feel	**Sentir**
Know	**Saber**
Leave	**Deixar, Sair**
Live	**Viver**
Make	**Fazer, preparar**
Meet	**Conhecer, Encontrar-se com**
Need	**Necessitar**
Pay	**Pagar**
Play	**Brincar / Jogar**
Remember	**Lembrar**
Repeat	**Repertir**
Say	**Dizer**
Sit	**Sentar-se**
Sleep	**Dormir**

17. Essential Verbs / Verbos Essenciais

Study	**Estudar**
Take	**Tomar**
Think	**Pensar**
Understand	**Compreender**
Wait	**Esperar**
Watch	**Olhar, Observar**
There is	**Há**
There are	**Há**
I am tall	**(Eu) sou alto**
You are short	**(Você) é pequeño**
He is thin	**Ele é magro**
We are big	**(Nós) somos grandes**
They are intelligent	**(Eles/as) são inteligentes**
I am at home	**(Eu) estou em casa**
You are at school	**(Você) está na escola**
We are at the store	**(Nós) estamos na loja**
I get a prize	**(Eu) obtenho um prêmio**
I go to the movies	**(Eu) vou ao cinema**
I have a nice car	**(Eu) tenho um bonito carro**
I listen to the music	**(Eu) escuto música**
I watch TV.	**(Eu) vejo a televisão**
I like this book	**Gosto deste livro**
There are ten children in the park	**Há dez crianças no parque**

18. Interrogative Words / Palavras Interrogativas

English	Portuguese
How many ...?	**Quantos/as...?**
How much...?	**Quanto/a...?**
How ...?	**Como...?**
What ...?	**Que...?**
When ...?	**Quando...?**
Where ...?	**Onde...?**
Which ...?	**Qual...?**
Who ...?	**Quem...?**
Whose ...?	**De quem...?**
Whom ...? / To whom ...?	**A quem...?**
Why ...?	**Por que?**
Because ...	**Porque?**

19. Linking Words / Conectores

English	Portuguese
And	**E**
But	**Mas**
Or	**Ou**
Either ... or	**Ou...Ou**
Neither ... nor	**Nem...Nem**
Yes	**Sim**
No	**Não**
So	**Então**
While	**Enquanto**

20. The Prepositions / As Preposições

About	**Sobre**
Above	**Em cima de**
Across	**Em frente de, ao largo**
At	**A, em**
Behind	**Detrás de**
Below	**Debaixo de**
Between	**Entre**
By	**De (meios de transporte), por**
Down	**Abaixo**
During	**Durante**
For	**Por, para**
From	**De, desde**
In	**Em, dentro de**
In front of	**Em frente de / diante de**
Into	**Dentro**

20. The Prepositions **/ As Preposições**

Near	**Perto**
Next to	**Junto de**
Of	**De**
On	**Em, sobre**
Out	**Fora**
Over	**Sobre, por em cima**
Per	**Por**
Through	**Através**
To	**Para(para alguém), até**
Under	**Debaixo**
Up	**Em cima**
With	**Com**
Without	**Sem**
The cat is in the box	**O gato está dentro da caixa**
The vase is on the table	**O vaso de flores está sobre a mesa**
Somebody is at the door	**Alguém está na porta**

21. Giving Directions / Dando instruções para chegar a um lugar

At the corner	**Na esquina**
Far	**Longe**
Near	**Perto**
Go straight ahead	**Continue tudo direto**
Left	**Esquerda**
Right	**Direita**
Turn left	**Dobre à esquerda**
Turn right	**Dobre à direita**
Go straight one block	**Continue direto um bloco mais**
After the traffic light, turn right	**Depois do semáforo, dobre à direita**
How can I get to ...?	**Como posso chegar a...?**
Where is the ...?	**Onde está o / a...?**
Where is the church?	**Onde fica a Igreja?**
The museum is next to the shopping center	**O museu está do lado do shopping**
The drugstore is in front of the building	**A farmácia está em frente do edificio**
The supermarket is near the park	**O supermercado está perto do parque**

22. The Ordinal Numbers / Os Numerais Ordinais

First	**Primeiro**
Second	**Segundo**
Third	**Terceiro**
Fourth	**Quarto**
Fifth	**Quinto**
Sixth	**Sexto**
Seventh	**Sétimo**
Eighth	**Oitavo**
Ninth	**Nono**
Tenth	**Décimo**
Eleventh	**Décimo primeiro**
Twelfth	**Décimo segundo**
Twentieth	**Vigésimo**
Thirtieth	**Trigésimo**
The first building	**O primeiro edificio**
The second floor	**O segundo andar**

23. Countries, Nationalities, and Languages / **Paises, Nacionalidades e Idiomas**

Brazil (Country)	**Brasil (País)**
Brazilian (Nationality)	**brasileiro/a (nacionalidade)**
Portuguese (Language)	**Português (idioma)**
Colombia	**Colômbia**
Colombian	**colombiano/a**
Spanish	**espanhol**
China	**China**
Chinese	**Chinês/chinesa**
Chinese	**Chinês**
England	**Inglaterra**
English	**inglês/a**
English	**inglês**
France	**França**
French	**francês/a**
French	**francês**
Germany	**Alemanha**
German	**alemão/alemã**
German	**alemão**
Italy	**Itália**

23. Countries, Nationalities, and Languages / **Paises, Nacionalidades e Idiomas**

Italian	**Italiano/a**
Italian	**Italiano/a**
Japan	**Japão**
Japanese	**japonês/a**
Japanese	**japonês**
Mexico	**México**
Mexican	**mexicano/a**
Spanish	**espanhol**
Spain	**Espanha**
Spanish	**espanhol/a**
Spanish	**espanhol**
United States of America (U.S.A.)	**Estados Unidos de América**
American	**americano/a**
English	**inglês**
Where are you from?	**De onde você é?**
I am from Brazil	**Eu sou do Brasil**
I am Brazilian	**Eu sou brasileiro**
I speak Portuguese	**Eu falo português**
I am not from Italy	**Eu não sou da Itália**

24. Indefinite Pronouns / **Pronomes Indefinidos**

Anybody	**Alguém (interrogativo), ninguém (negativo)**
Anything	**Alguma coisa (interrogativo), nada (negativo)**
Nobody	**Ninguém**
Nothing	**Nada**
Somebody	**Alguém (afirmativo)**
Something	**Alguma coisa (afirmativo)**
Everybody	**Todos**
Everything	**Tudo**
Is anybody home?	**Tem alguém em casa?**
I don't want anything	**Não quero nada**
Nothing happened	**Não aconteceu nada**
Somebody is in the living room	**Alguém está na sala**
Everything is ready	**Tudo está pronto**

25. The Emotions / As Emoções

Angry	**Com raiva, chateado**
Bored	**Entediado**
Confident	**Seguro de si mesmo**
Confused	**Confuso**
Embarrassed	**Envergonhado**
Excited	**Entusiasmado**
Happy	**Contente**
Nervous	**Nervoso**
Proud	**Orgulhoso**
Sad	**Triste**
Scared	**Assustado**
Shy	**Tímido**
Surprised	**Surpreendido**
Worried	**Preocupado**
I am happy	**(Eu)estou contente**
He is sad	**Ele está triste**
They are surprised	**Eles estão surpreendidos**
Are you excited?	**Você está entusiasmada?**
I am not bored	**(Eu)não estou entediado**
She is not nervous	**Ela não está nervosa**
Everybody is confident	**Todos estão seguros de si mesmos**

26. Adverbs / Advérbios

A few	**Uns poucos**
A little	**Um pouco**
A lot	**Muito**
After	**Depois**
Again	**Outra vez**
Ago	**Atrás**
Also	**Também**
Always	**Sempre**
Before	**Antes**
Enough	**Suficientemente**
Everyday	**Todos os dias**
Exactly	**exatamente**
Finally	**Finalmente**
First	**Em primeiro lugar**
Here	**aquí**
Late	**Tarde**
Later	**Mais tarde**
Never	**Nunca**
Next	**Próximo**
Now	**Agora**

26. Adverbs / **Advérbios**

Often	**Freqüentemente**
Once	**Uma vez**
Only	**Somente**
Outside	**Fora**
Really	**Realmente**
Right here	**Aquí mesmo**
Right now	**Agora mesmo**
Since	**Desde**
Slowly	**Lentamente**
Sometimes	**Às vezes**
Soon	**Em breve**
Still	**Ainda**
Then	**Logo**
There	**Lá**
Today	**Hoje**
Tomorrow	**Amanhã**
Tonight	**Esta noite**
Too	**Também**
Usually	**Geralmente**

27. Auxiliary Verbs / Verbos Auxiliares

Can	**Poder (para habilidades e pedidos informais)**
Could	**Poder (para pedidos formais)**
Did	**∅**
Do	**Fazer (auxiliar para o presente simples)**
Does	**Fazer (auxiliar para o presente simples - terceira pessoa)**
Have to	**Ter que**
May	**Poder (para pedir licença)**
Must	**Dever (obrigação)**
Should	**Dever (para dar conselhos)**
Will	**∅**
Would	**∅**
Can you go to the movies?	**Você pode ir ao cinema?**
Could I have change?	**Você poderia me dar dinheiro trocado?**
Did you work at the drugstore?	**Trabalhaste na farmácia?**
I did not (didn't) work at the drugstore	**(Eu) trabalhei na farmácia**
Do you work at the drugstore?	**Trabalhas na farmácia?**
I do not (don't) work at the drugstore	**(Eu) não trabalho na farmácia**
Does he read the newspaper?	**Ele lê o jornal?**
He does not (doesn't) read the newspaper	**Ele não lê o jornal**
I have to do my homework	**(Eu) tenho que fazer a minha tarefa.**
May I help you?	**Posso lhe ajudar?**
You must turn left now	**(Você) deve dobrar à esquerda agora**
You should go to the doctor	**(Você) deveria ir ao doutor**
I will work tomorrow	**(Eu) trabalharei amanhã**
I would like a glass of wine	**(Eu) gostaria de uma taça de vinho**

28. Expressions / Espressões

All right	**Está bem**
Come in	**Entre**
Come here, please	**Venha por aquí, por favor**
Don't worry!	**Não te preocupes!**
For example	**Por exemplo**
Good luck!	**Boa sorte!**
Great idea!	**Exelente idéia!**
Have a nice day!	**Que tenha um bom dia!**
Help yourself!	**Sírva-se alguma coisa!**
Here you are	**Aquí tens**
Hurry up!	**Mais depressa**
I agree	**Concordo**
I disagree	**Não concordo**
I don't care	**Não me importo**
I don't know	**Não sei**
I'm coming!	**Já vou**
I'm afraid...	**Tenho medo de que...**
It's a deal!	**Trato feito!**
Keep well!	**Que você continue estando bem!**
Let me think	**Deixe-me pensar**
Let's go!	**Vamos!**
Right now	**Neste momento**
Sounds good!	**Soa bem**
Sure	**Com certeza**
Take a seat	**Sente-se**
Take care!	**Cuide-se!**

29. The Family / A Família

Father	**O pai**
Mother	**A mãe**
Son	**O filho**
Daughter	**A filha**
Brother	**O irmão**
Sister	**A irmã**
Grandfather	**O avô**
Grandmother	**A avó**
Uncle	**O tio**
Aunt	**A tia**
Cousin	**O primo/a**
Nephew	**O sobrinho**
Niece	**A sobrinha**
Husband	**O esposo**
Wife	**A esposa**
Boyfriend	**O namorado**
Girlfriend	**A namorada**
In-laws	**Os parentes políticos**
Father in-law	**O sogro**
Mother in-law	**A sogra**
Brother in-law	**O cunhado**
Sister in-law	**A cunhada**
Step father	**O padrasto**
Step mother	**A madrasta**
Step brother	**O irmão de criação**
Step sister	**A irmã de criação**
Who is he?	**Quem é ele?**
He is my brother	**Ele é meu irmão**

30. The House / A casa

Living room	**A sala**
Door	**A porta**
Window	**A janela**
Sofa	**O sofá**
Lamp	**A lâmpada**
Dining room	**sala de jantar**
Table	**A mesa**
Chair	**A cadeira**
Kitchen	**A cozinha**
Stove	**O aquecedor**
Oven	**O forno**
Fridge	**A geladeira**
Microwave	**O microonda**
Bedroom	**O quarto**
Bed	**A cama**
Nightstand	**A mesa de cabeceira**
Vanity	**Cómoda com espelho**
Chest of drawers	**A cómoda**
Closet	**O guarda-roupa**
Bathroom	**O banheiro**
Mirror	**O espelho**
Sink	**A pia**
Toilet	**O sanitário**
Bathtub	**A bacia**
Laundry room	**A lavanderia**
Driveway	**O estacionamento**
Where is the living room?	**Onde está a sala?**
The door is big	**A porta é grande**
The stove is small	**O aquecedor é pequeño**
The kitchen is beautiful	**A cozinha é bonita**

31. The City **/ A Cidade**

Block	**O bloco**
Building	**O edificio**
Church	**A igreja**
Movie theater	**O cinema**
Museum	**O museu**
Park	**O parque**
Drugstore	**A farmácia**
Restaurant	**O restaurante**
Shopping center	**O shopping**
Store	**A loja**
Street	**A rua**
Supermarket	**O supermercado**

32. At the Supermarket / No Supermercado

The food	**Os alimentos**
The fruits	**As frutas**
Apple	**A maçã**
Banana	**A banana**
Cherry	**A cereja**
Grapes	**As uvas**
Orange	**A laranja**
Strawberry	**O morango**
The vegetables	**Os vegetais**
Beans	**Os feijões**
Carrot	**A cenoura**
Cauliflower	**O couve-flor**
Lettuce	**O alface**
Onion	**Cebola**
Pepper	**O pimentão**
Potato	**A batata**
Tomato	**O tomate**
The meats	**As carnes**
Beef	**A carne de vaca**
Chicken	**A carne de frango**
Turkey	**O perú**
Ham	**O presunto**
Pork	**A carne de porco**
The dairy products	**Os produtos lácteos**
Butter	**A manteiga**
Cheese	**O queijo**
Milk	**O leite**

32. At the Supermarket / No Supermercado

Yogurt	**O iogurte**
Jam	**A geléia**
Bread	**O pão**
Eggs	**Os ovos**
Fish	**O peixe**
Seafood	**Os mariscos**
Can	**A lata**
Cart	**O carrinho**
Bag	**A bolsa**
Basket	**A cesta**
Bottle	**A garrafa**
Cash register	**A caixa registradora**
Cashier	**Ele / ela caixa**
Customer service	**Serviço ao cliente**
Groceries	**As compras**
How many...?	**Quantos/as...?**
How many oranges do you buy?	**Quantas laranjas você compra?**
How much does it cost?	**Quanto custa...?**
How much do the bananas cost?	**Quanto custam as bananas?**
I want...	**Eu quero...**
I want to buy a bottle of milk	**Eu quero comprar uma garrafa de leite**
I would like...	**Eu gostaria.../queria...**
I would like a bag of tomatoes	**Eu queria uma bolsa de tomates**
Where is the lettuce?	**Onde está o alface?**
It's on aisle one	**Está na seção um**
Where are the cans of vegetables?	**Onde estão as latas dos vegetais?**
They are on aisle five	**Estão na seção cinco**

33. At the Restaurant / No Restaurante

Waiter / waitress	**O garçom/a garçonete**
Breakfast	**Café-da manhã**
Lunch	**Almoço**
Dinner	**Janta**
To eat	**Comer**
To drink	**Beber**
To eat breakfast	**Tomar o café-da manhã**
The menu	**A carta**
Appetizer	**O aperitivo**
Salad	**A salada**
Soup	**A sopa**
Main course	**O prato principal**
Pasta	**As massas**
Rice	**O arroz**
French fries	**As batatas fritas**
Mashed potatoes	**O purê de batatas**
Baked potatoes	**As batatas ao forno**
Barbecue	**O churrasco**
Fried chicken	**O frango frito**
Steak	**A bisteca**

33. At the Restaurant / No Restaurante

Dessert	**A sobremesa**
Beverages	**As bebidas**
Coffee	**O café**
Tea	**O chá**
Soda	**A bebida com gás**
Lemonade	**A limonada**
Orange juice	**O suco de laranja**
Alcoholic drinks	**As bebidas alcoólicas**
Beer	**A cerveja**
Wine	**O vinho**
Check	**A conta**
Tip	**A gorjeta**
How may I help you?	**Como posso lhe ajudar?**
What would you like to order?	**O que você deseja?**
May I have the menu, please?	**Você pode me dar o menu, por favor?**
Could I get more water, please?	**Você poderia me trazer mais água, por favor?**
My order is wrong	**Esta não é a minha ordem**
The service here is wonderful!	**O serviço daquí é exelente!**
The food is delicious!	**A comida está deliciosa!**
The check, please	**A conta, por favor**
The tip is included	**A gorgeta está incluida**

34. The Office / A Oficina

Book	**O livro**
Calculator	**A calculadora**
Computer	**O computador**
Desk	**Mesa de oficina**
Fax machine	**A máquina de fax**
File	**O expediente**
File cabinet	**O arquivador**
Folder	**A pasta**
Keyboard	**O techado**
Monitor	**O monitor**
Mouse	**O mouse**
Notebook	**O caderno**
Pad	**O bloco**
Paper	**O papel**
Pen	**A caneta**
Printer	**A impressora**
Ruler	**A régua**
Scissors	**A tesoura**
Screen	**A tela**
Stapler	**O grampeador**
Telephone	**O telefone**
My computer is broken	**Meu computador está rebentado**
There is no paper in the printer	**Não tem papel na impressora**
We need to buy more folders	**Precisamos comprar mais pastas**
We don't have a copy machine	**Não temos fotocopiadora**

35. Jobs and Positions / Os Trabalhos e os Postos

Accountant	**O contador/A contadora**
Architect	**O arquiteto**
Artist	**O artista**
Chef	**O chef de cozinha**
Clerk	**O empregado/A empregada**
Cook	**O cozinheiro/ A cozinheira**
Doctor	**O doutor/ A doutora**
Engineer	**O engenheiro**
Gardener	**O jardineiro**
Graphic designer	**O designer gráfico/ A designer gráfico**
Lawyer	**O advogado**
Nurse	**O enfermeiro/ A enfermeira**
Physician	**O médico**
Salesperson	**O vendedor/ A vendedora**
Secretary	**A secretária**
Security guard	**O guarda de segurança**
Taxi driver	**O taxista**
Teacher	**O professor/ A professora**
Technician	**O técnico**
Tourist guide	**O guia turístico**
Travel agent	**O agente de viagens**

36. Job Interview / A Entrevista de Trabalho

Apply for a job	**Pedir emprego**
Duty	**Tarefa**
Experience	**Esxperiência**
Last name	**Sobrenome**
First name	**Nome**
Full time job	**Trabalho em tempo integral**
Part time job	**Trabalho de meia jornada**
Résumé	**Currículum vitae**
Skill	**Habilidade**
Work	**Trabalhar / O trabalho**

37. The Transportation / Os Meios de Transporte

Airplane	**O avião**
Bicycle	**A bicicleta**
Bus	**O ônibus**
Car	**O automóvel**
Helicopter	**O helicóptero**
Metro	**O metrô**
Motorcycle	**A moto**
Train	**O trem**
Truck	**O caminhão**

38. The Traffic / O Trânsito

Bus stop	**A parada de ônibus**
Crosswalk	**A faixa para pedestres**
Freeway, highway	**A rodovia**
Gas station	**O posto de gasolina**
Intersection	**O cruzamento de ruas**
Lane	**A faixa (de uma rodovia)**
No outlet	**O caminho sem saída**
One way	**Um só sentido**
Pedestrian	**O pedestre**
Speed	**A velocidade**
Stop sign	**O sinal de stop**
To get in	**Subir, entrar**
To get off	**Descer, sair**
Toll	**O pedágio**
Traffic light	**O semáforo**
Train station	**A estação ferroviária**
Two way	**Duas vias**
U-turn	**Girar em U**
Yield	**Dar passo**
I get in the car	**(Eu) subo no carro**
I get off the car	**(Eu) desço do carro**
We wait for the train	**(Nós) esperamos o trem**

39. The Car / O Automóvel

Accelerator	**O acelerador**
Battery	**A bateria**
Hood	**O capô**
Brake	**O freio**
Clutch	**A embreagem**
Engine	**O motor**
Fender	**O pára-choques**
Gear box	**A caixa de velocidades**
Headlight	**A luz**
Rear view mirror	**O espelho retrovisor**
Make	**A marca**
Model	**O modelo**
Radiator	**O radiador**
Steering wheel	**O volante**
Seat	**O assento**
Tire	**O pneu**
Trunk	**O porta-mala**
Wheel	**A roda**
Windshield	**O pára-brisas**
Windshield wipers	**O limpa pára-brisas**
The car is broken	**O carro está quebrado**
I have a flat tire	**Desinchou um pneu**
I need a new battery	**Preciso de uma bateria nova**
What year is the car?	**De que ano é o carro?**
What make is the car?	**Qual a marca do carro?**
What model is the car?	**Qual o modelo do carro?**
How many miles does the car have?	**Quantos kilômetros tem o carro?**

40. Phone Conversations / Conversas Telefônicas

Call	**Ligar**
Dial	**Discar**
Directory	**A guia telefônica**
Directory Assistance	**A informação**
Extension	**O número interno**
Hold on, please	**Não desligue, por favor/ Um momento, por favor**
I'd like to speak to...	**Queria falar com...**
I'll put you through	**Lhe comunicarei**
I'll transfer your call	**Transferirei sua ligação**
I'm calling about ...	**Ligo por...**
Just a minute	**Espere um minuto**
Leave a message	**Deixar uma mensagem**
Let me see...	**Deixe-me ver**
Phone	**Telefone/ Ligar**
Phone number	**Número de telefone**
Ring	**Soar**
Speak	**Falar**
Speaking	**Fala ele/ela**
Take a message	**escrever uma mensagem**
Talk	**Falar**
This is...	**Sou / Fala...**
Who's calling?	**Quem é / Quem fala**

41. At the Post Office / Nos Correios

English	Portuguese
Air mail	**Correio aéreo**
Counter	**O balcão**
Envelope	**O envelope**
Letter	**A carta**
Mail	**A correspondência**
Parcel	**O pacote**
Postcard	**O cartão postal**
Postman, mailman	**O carteiro**
Stamp	**O selo**
To send	**Enviar**
To deliver	**Entregar**
Delivery	**A entrega**
To pick up	**retirar**
Address	**O endereço**
I want to send a letter	**Quero enviar uma carta**
I would like to pick up a parcel	**Gostaris de retirar um pacote**
How much do the stamps cost?	**Quanto custam os selos?**
Do you sell postcards?	**Vocês vendem cartões postais?**

42. At the Bank / No Banco

Account	**A conta**
ATM	**A caixa eletrônica**
Bank statement	**O resume bancário**
Bank teller	**O / A caixa**
Cash	**O dinheiro**
Checkbook	**O talão de cheques**
Checking account	**A conta corrente**
Credit card	**O cartão de crédito**
Debit card	**O cartão de débito**
Deposit slip	**O comprovante de depósito**
Savings account	**A caderneta de poupança**
To deposit	**Depositar**
To save	**Poupar**
To transfer	**Transferir**
To withdraw	**Retirar**
Transactions	**As transações**
Withdrawal slip	**O comprovante de retiro**
I want to make a deposit	**Quero fazer um depósito**
Do you have a savings account?	**Você tem uma conta poupança?**
I have a checking account	**Tenho uma conta corrente**
What is your credit card number?	**Qual o número do seu cartão de crédito?**
I don't have an ATM card	**Não tenho cartão do caixa eletrônico**
Where are the deposit slips?	**Onde estão os comprovantes de depósito?**

43. At the Airport / No Aeroporto

Arrival	**A chegada**
Concourse	**O corredor**
Customs	**A alfândega**
Departure	**A partida**
Destination	**O destino**
Entrance	**A entrada**
Exit	**A saída**
First class	**Primeira classe**
Flight	**O vôo**
Gate	**A porta**
Immigrations office	**A oficina de Imigrações**
Luggage	**A equipagem**
Passport	**O passaporte**
Restrooms	**Os banheiros**
Suitcase	**A mala**
To arrive	**Chegar**
To depart	**Partir**
To travel	**Viajar**
Trip	**A viagem**
Where are you traveling?	**Para onde você vai viajar?**
May I have your ticket, please?	**Pode me dar a sua passagem?**
I need you passport, please	**Preciso do seu passaporte, por favor**
My flight number is ...	**Meu número de vôo é...**
Where is gate number ...?	**Onde está a porta de número...**
The flight is delayed	**O vôo está atrasado**
The flight is on time	**O vôo está a tempo**

44. At the Hotel **/ No Hotel**

Double room	**O quarto com duas camas**
Single room	**O quarto com uma cama**
Bell desk	**O porteiro**
Bellman	**O auxiliar de serviços**
Elevator	**O elevador**
Reception	**A recepção**
Receptionist	**O / A recepcionista**
Reservation	**A reserva**
Stairway	**As escadas**
Swimming pool	**A piscina**
Tours desk	**O posto de turismo**
Valet parking	**O serviço de estacionamento**
To check-in	**Registrar-se**
To check-out	**Pagar a conta do hotel**
I would like to make a reservation	**Gostaria de fazer uma reserva**
I want a single room	**Quero um quarto com uma cama**
I would like to check-in	**Eu gostaria de me registrar**

45. The Clothes / A Roupa

Bathing suit	**A roupa de banho / O biquini**
Belt	**O cinto**
Blouse	**A blusa**
Coat	**O casaco**
Dress	**O vestido**
Gloves	**As luvas**
Hat	**O chapéu**
Jacket	**A jaqueta**
Pants	**As calças**
Purse	**A carteira**
Scarf	**O cachecol**
Shirt	**A camisa**
Shoes	**Os sapatos**
Shorts	**Os shorts**
Skirt	**A saia**
Socks	**As meias**
Suit	**O terno**
Suitcase	**A mala**
The size	**O tamanho**
Small	**Pequeño**
Medium	**Médio**
Large	**Grande**
Big sizes	**Tamanhos grandes**

46. At the Shopping Center / No Shopping

Department store	**Seção, Departamento**
Ladies	**Senhoras**
Men	**Senhores**
Juniors	**Jovens**
Kids	**Crianças**
Ladies' department	**Seção de senhoras**
Jewelry	**Joalheria**
Fitting room	**Provador**
Elevator	**Elevador**
Escalator	**Escada mecânica**
How may I help you?	**Como posso lhe ajudar?**
I'm looking for ...	**Estou buscando...**
I'm just looking	**Só estou olhando**
Where is the fitting room?	**Onde está o provador?**
It fits well	**Fica bem em mim**
It doesn't fit well	**Não fica muito bem em mim**
May I pay here?	**Posso pagar aquí?**
I want to exchange this	**Quero mudar esto**
I want to return this	**Quero devolver esto**
I like ...	**Eu gosto...**
I like this blouse	**Gosto desta blusa**
I don't like ...	**Eu não gosto...**
I don't like these pants	**Eu não gosto desta calça**

47. At the Drugstore / Na Farmácia

Antiseptic	**O desinfetante**
Adhesive bandage	**O band-aid**
Antibiotic	**O antibiótico**
Aspirin	**A aspirina**
Bandage	**O curativo**
Cold medicine	**O remédio para o resfriado**
Cough syrup	**O xarope para a tosse**
Medication	**Os remédios**
Ointment	**A pomada**
OTC (Over The Counter) medication	**Os remédios sem receita**
Painkiller	**O calmante**
Pills	**Os comprimidos**
Prescription	**A receita médica**
Tablets	**As tabelas**
Thermometer	**O termômetro**
Cotton	**O algodão**

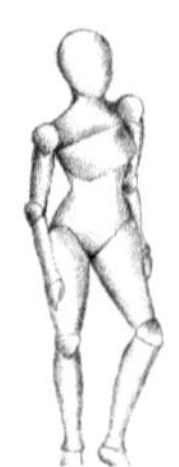

48. The Parts of the Body **/ As parte do Corpo**

Ankle	**O tornozelo**
Arm	**O braço**
Back	**As costas**
Buttock	**A bunda**
Calf	**Panturrilha**
Chest	**O peito**
Elbow	**O cotovelo**
Feet	**Os pés**
Finger	**O dedo da mão**
Foot	**O pé**
Forearm	**Antebraço**
Hand	**A mão**
Head	**A cabeça**
Hip	**O quadril**
Knee	**O joelho**
Leg	**A perna**
Neck	**O pescoço**
Shoulder	**O ombro**
Stomach	**O estômago**
Thigh	**A coxa**
Toe	**O dedo do pé**
Waist	**A cintura**
Wrist	**O pulso**

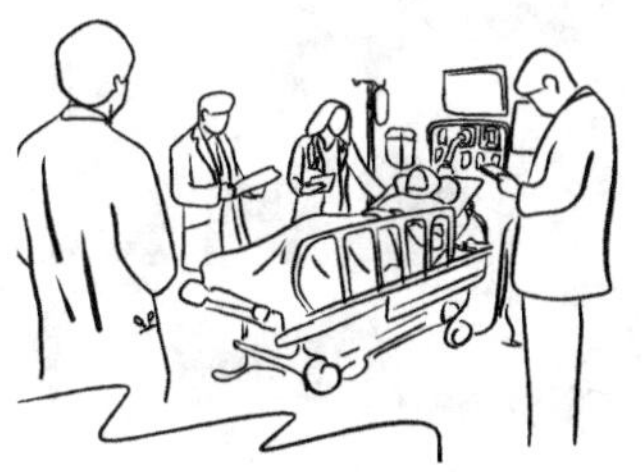

49. Health Problems / Problemas de Saúde

Backache	**Dor nas costas**
Cold	**O resfriado**
Fever	**A febre**
Hurt	**Ferir-se, magoar-se, machucar-se**
Indigestion	**A indigestão**
Injury	**A ferida**
Pain	**A dor**
Pulse	**O pulso**
Sick	**Doente**
Sneeze	**O espirro**
Sore throat	**A dor de garganta**
Toothache	**A dor de dente**
I have a headache	**Tenho dor de cabeça**
I have a stomachache	**Tenho dor de estômago**
I have pain in my knee	**Dói o meu joelho**
I hurt my hand	**Machuquei a minha mão**
I've got a cold	**Tenho um resfriado**
My foot hurts	**Dói o meu pé**

50. The Animals / Os Animais

Bear	**O urso**
Bird	**O pássaro**
Cat	**O gato**
Chicken	**O frango**
Cow	**A vaca**
Dog	**O cachorro**
Duck	**O pato**
Elephant	**O elefante**
Fish	**O peixe**
Horse	**O cavalo**
Lizard	**A lagartixa**
Lion	**O leão**
Monkey	**O macaco**
Mouse	**O rato**
Rat	**O rato**
Tiger	**O tigre**

EXERCISE!

Write the Portuguese translation.

Keep practicing at:

QuickLanguages.com

1. Greetings **/ Cumprimentos**

English	Portuguese
Hi! / Hello!	Olá!
Good morning	
Good afternoon	
Good evening / Good night	
How are you doing?	
Fine	
Very well	
Thank you / Thanks	
Thank you very much	
You're welcome	
Fine, thank you	
And you?	
See you	
See you later	
See you tomorrow	
Goodbye	
Bye	

2. Introductions and Courtesy Expressions **/ Apresentações e Expressões de Cortesia**

What is your name?	Qual o seu nome?
My name is ...	
Who are you?	
I am ...	
Who is he / she?	
He is ... / She is ...	
Nice to meet you / Pleased to meet you	
Nice to meet you, too	
It's my pleasure	
Excuse me	
Please	
One moment, please	
Welcome	
Go ahead	
Can you repeat, please?	
I don't understand	
I understand a little	
Can you speak more slowly, please?	
Do you speak Spanish?	
How do you say hello in Spanish?	
What does it mean?	
I speak Spanish a little	

3. Ways to Address to a Person / Maneiras de se Dirigir a uma Pessoa

Madam / Ma'am	Senhora
Miss	
Ms.	
Mr.	
Mrs.	
Sir	
Dr.	

4. The Articles / Os Artigos

The	O / a / os / as
The car	
The cars	
The house	
The houses	
A	
A car	
A house	
An	
An elephant	
An apple	
Some	
Some cars	
Some houses	

5. The Subject Pronouns **/ Os Pronomes Pessoais de Sujeito**

English	Portuguese
I	Eu
You	
He	
She	
It	
We	
You	
They	

6. The Possessive Adjectives **/ Os Adjetivos Possessivos**

English	Portuguese
My	Mim
Your	
His	
Her	
Its	
Our	
Your	
Their	
My car	
Your book	
His TV	
Our house	

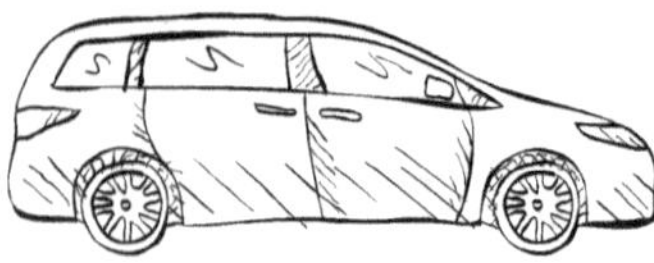

7. The Demonstrative Adjectives / **Os Adjetivos Demonstrativos**

This	Este / esta
This book	
This shirt	
These	
These books	
These shirts	
That	
That table	
That car	
Those	
Those tables	
Those cars	

8. The Possessive Pronouns / **Os Pronomes Possessivos**

Mine	Meu
Yours	
His	
Hers	
Its	
Ours	
Yours	
Theirs	
The car is mine	
The book is yours	
That TV is his	
This house is ours	

9. The Cardinal Numbers / **Os Numerais Cardinais**

0 / Zero Zero

1 / One

2 / Two

3 / Three

4 / Four

5 / Five

6 / Six

7 / Seven

8 / Eight

9 / Nine

10 / Ten

11 / Eleven

12 / Twelve

13 / Thirteen

14 / Fourteen

15 / Fifteen

16 / Sixteen

17 / Seventeen

18 / Eighteen

19 / Nineteen

20 / Twenty

21 / Twenty-one

30 / Thirty

40 / Forty

50 / Fifty

60 / Sixty

9. The Cardinal Numbers / **Os Numerais Cardinais**

70 / Seventy	Setenta
80 / Eighty	
90 /Ninety	
100 / One hundred	
101 / One hundred and one	
200 / Two hundred	
300 / Three hundred	
400 / Four hundred	
500 / Five hundred	
600 / Six hundred	
700 / Seven hundred	
800 / Eight hundred	
900 /Nine hundred	
1,000 / One thousand	
10,000 / Ten thousand	
100,000 / One hundred thousand	
1,000,000 / One million	
1,000,000,000 / One billion	
Forty-five (45)	
One hundred and twenty-eight (128)	
One thousand nine hundred and sixty-three (1,963)	
Six thousand and thirty-seven (6,037)	
Eleven thousand (11,000)	
Two hundred and seventy-nine thousand (279,000)	
Two million (2,000,000)	

10. The Time
/ **A Hora**

English	Portuguese
The clock	O relógio (de pared)
The watch	
What time is it?	
It is ...	
It is one o'clock (1:00)	
It is two o'clock (2:00)	
It is three fifteen / It is a quarter past three (3:15)	
It is four thirty / It is half past four (4:30)	
It is five forty-five / It is a quarter to six (5:45)	
It is six fifty / It is ten to seven (6:50)	
It is noon (12:00 P. M.)	
It is midnight (12:00 A. M.)	
In the morning	
In the afternoon	
In the evening	
At night	
At what time is ...?	
At what time is the concert?	
At ...	
At 7:10 P.M. (seven ten in the evening)	

11. The Days of the Week **/ Os Dias da Semana**

Monday	Segunda-feira
Tuesday	
Wednesday	
Thursday	
Friday	
Saturday	
Sunday	
What day is today?	

12. The Months of the Year **/ Os Meses do Ano**

January	Janeiro
February	
March	
April	
May	
June	
July	
August	
September	
October	
November	
December	
What is today's date?	

13. The Weather / O Clima

Sunny	Ensolarado
Cloudy	
Rainy	
Humid	
Dry	
Cold	
Warm	
Hot	
Rain	
Snow	
How is the weather today?	
It's nice	
It's sunny	
It's cold in winter	
It's raining	
It's snowing	
I am cold	

14. The Seasons / As Estações

Spring	Primavera
Summer	
Fall	
Winter	

15. The Colors / As Cores

Yellow	Amarelo
Red	
Blue	
Green	
Orange	
Brown	
Pink	
Purple	
Black	
White	
Gray	
Light	
Dark	
Light green	
Orange book	
Brown shoes	
My blouse is white	
What color is...?	
What is your favorite color?	

16. The Parts of the Face **/ As Partes da Casa**

Cheek	A bochecha
Chin	
Ear	
Eye	
Forehead	
Hair	
Lips	
Mouth	
Nose	
Skin	
Teeth	
Tooth	
Blond / Blonde	
Brown	
Gray	
Red hair	
Long	
Short	
Straight	
Curly	
John is blond	
Karen has long hair	
He has green eyes	
Her eyes are blue	
His eyes are big and brown	

17. Essential Verbs **/ Verbos Essenciais**

Be	Ser / Estar
Go	
Come	
Have	
Get	
Help	
Love	
Like	
Want	
Buy	
Sell	
Read	
Write	
Drink	
Eat	
Open	
Close	
Look at	
Look for	
Find	
Start	
Stop	
Pull	

17. Essential Verbs / **Verbos Essenciais**

Push Empurrar

Send

Receive

Turn on

Turn off

Listen to

Speak

Do

Drive

Feel

Know

Leave

Live

Make

Meet

Need

Pay

Play

Remember

Repeat

Say

Sit

Sleep

17. Essential Verbs / **Verbos Essenciais**

Study	Estudar
Take	
Think	
Understand	
Wait	
Watch	
There is	
There are	
I am tall	
You are short	
He is thin	
We are big	
They are intelligent	
I am at home	
You are at school	
We are at the store	
I get a prize	
I go to the movies	
I have a nice car	
I listen to the music	
I watch TV.	
I like this book	
There are ten children in the park	

18. Interrogative Words **/ Palavras Interrogativas**

How many ...?	Quantos/as...?
How much...?	
How ...?	
What ...?	
When ...?	
Where ...?	
Which ...?	
Who ...?	
Whose ...?	
Whom ...? / To whom ...?	
Why ...?	
Because ...	

19. Linking Words **/ Conectores**

And	E
But	
Or	
Either ... or	
Neither ... nor	
Yes	
No	
So	
While	

20. The Prepositions / As Preposições

About	Sobre
Above	
Across	
At	
Behind	
Below	
Between	
By	
Down	
During	
For	
From	
In	
In front of	
Into	

20. The Prepositions **/ As Preposições**

Near	Perto
Next to	
Of	
On	
Out	
Over	
Per	
Through	
To	
Under	
Up	
With	
Without	
The cat is in the box	
The vase is on the table	
Somebody is at the door	

21. Giving Directions **/ Dando instruções para chegar a um lugar**

At the corner	Na esquina
Far	
Near	
Go straight ahead	
Left	
Right	
Turn left	
Turn right	
Go straight one block	
After the traffic light, turn right	
How can I get to ...?	
Where is the ...?	
Where is the church?	
The museum is next to the shopping center	
The drugstore is in front of the building	
The supermarket is near the park	

22. The Ordinal Numbers / Os Numerais Ordinais

First	Primeiro
Second	
Third	
Fourth	
Fifth	
Sixth	
Seventh	
Eighth	
Ninth	
Tenth	
Eleventh	
Twelfth	
Twentieth	
Thirtieth	
The first building	
The second floor	

23. Countries, Nationalities, and Languages **/ Paises, Nacionalidades e Idiomas**

Brazil (Country)	Brasil (País)
Brazilian (Nationality)	
Portuguese (Language)	
Colombia	
Colombian	
Spanish	
China	
Chinese	
Chinese	
England	
English	
English	
France	
French	
French	
Germany	
German	
German	
Italy	

23. Countries, Nationalities, and Languages / **Paises, Nacionalidades e Idiomas**

Italian	Italiano/a
Italian	
Japan	
Japanese	
Japanese	
Mexico	
Mexican	
Spanish	
Spain	
Spanish	
Spanish	
United States of America (U.S.A.)	
American	
English	
Where are you from?	
I am from Brazil	
I am Brazilian	
I speak Portuguese	
I am not from Italy	

24. Indefinite Pronouns / Pronomes Indefinidos

Anybody	Alguém (interrogativo), ninguém (negativo)
Anything	
Nobody	
Nothing	
Somebody	
Something	
Everybody	
Everything	
Is anybody home?	
I don't want anything	
Nothing happened	
Somebody is in the living room	
Everything is ready	

25. The Emotions
/ As Emoções

Angry	Com raiva, chateado
Bored	
Confident	
Confused	
Embarrassed	
Excited	
Happy	
Nervous	
Proud	
Sad	
Scared	
Shy	
Surprised	
Worried	
I am happy	
He is sad	
They are surprised	
Are you excited?	
I am not bored	
She is not nervous	
Everybody is confident	

26. Adverbs / Advérbios

A few	Uns poucos
A little	
A lot	
After	
Again	
Ago	
Also	
Always	
Before	
Enough	
Everyday	
Exactly	
Finally	
First	
Here	
Late	
Later	
Never	
Next	
Now	

26. Adverbs
/ Advérbios

Often	Freqüentemente
Once	
Only	
Outside	
Really	
Right here	
Right now	
Since	
Slowly	
Sometimes	
Soon	
Still	
Then	
There	
Today	
Tomorrow	
Tonight	
Too	
Usually	

27. Auxiliary Verbs / Verbos Auxiliares

English	Portuguese
Can	Poder (para habilidades e pedidos informais)
Could	
Did	
Do	
Does	
Have to	
May	
Must	
Should	
Will	
Would	
Can you go to the movies?	
Could I have change?	
Did you work at the drugstore?	
I did not (didn't) work at the drugstore	
Do you work at the drugstore?	
I do not (don't) work at the drugstore	
Does he read the newspaper?	
He does not (doesn't) read the newspaper	
I have to do my homework	
May I help you?	
You must turn left now	
You should go to the doctor	
I will work tomorrow	
I would like a glass of wine	

28. Expressions **/ Espressões**

English	Portuguese
All right	Está bem
Come in	
Come here, please	
Don't worry!	
For example	
Good luck!	
Great idea!	
Have a nice day!	
Help yourself!	
Here you are	
Hurry up!	
I agree	
I disagree	
I don't care	
I don't know	
I'm coming!	
I'm afraid...	
It's a deal!	
Keep well!	
Let me think	
Let's go!	
Right now	
Sounds good!	
Sure	
Take a seat	
Take care!	

29. The Family / A Família

Father	O pai
Mother	
Son	
Daughter	
Brother	
Sister	
Grandfather	
Grandmother	
Uncle	
Aunt	
Cousin	
Nephew	
Niece	
Husband	
Wife	
Boyfriend	
Girlfriend	
In-laws	
Father in-law	
Mother in-law	
Brother in-law	
Sister in-law	
Step father	
Step mother	
Step brother	
Step sister	
Who is he?	
He is my brother	

30. The House / **A casa**

Living room	A sala
Door	
Window	
Sofa	
Lamp	
Dining room	
Table	
Chair	
Kitchen	
Stove	
Oven	
Fridge	
Microwave	
Bedroom	
Bed	
Nightstand	
Vanity	
Chest of drawers	
Closet	
Bathroom	
Mirror	
Sink	
Toilet	
Bathtub	
Laundry room	
Driveway	
Where is the living room?	
The door is big	
The stove is small	
The kitchen is beautiful	

31. The City **/ A Cidade**

Block	O bloco
Building	
Church	
Movie theater	
Museum	
Park	
Drugstore	
Restaurant	
Shopping center	
Store	
Street	
Supermarket	

32. At the Supermarket **/ No Supermercado**

The food	Os alimentos
The fruits	
Apple	
Banana	
Cherry	
Grapes	
Orange	
Strawberry	
The vegetables	
Beans	
Carrot	
Cauliflower	
Lettuce	
Onion	
Pepper	
Potato	
Tomato	
The meats	
Beef	
Chicken	
Turkey	
Ham	
Pork	
The dairy products	
Butter	
Cheese	
Milk	

32. At the Supermarket / No Supermercado

English	Portuguese
Yogurt	O iogurte
Jam	
Bread	
Eggs	
Fish	
Seafood	
Can	
Cart	
Bag	
Basket	
Bottle	
Cash register	
Cashier	
Customer service	
Groceries	
How many...?	
How many oranges do you buy?	
How much does it cost?	
How much do the bananas cost?	
I want...	
I want to buy a bottle of milk	
I would like...	
I would like a bag of tomatoes	
Where is the lettuce?	
It's on aisle one	
Where are the cans of vegetables?	
They are on aisle five	

33. At the Restaurant / No Restaurante

Waiter / waitress	O garçom/a garçonete
Breakfast	
Lunch	
Dinner	
To eat	
To drink	
To eat breakfast	
The menu	
Appetizer	
Salad	
Soup	
Main course	
Pasta	
Rice	
French fries	
Mashed potatoes	
Baked potatoes	
Barbecue	
Fried chicken	
Steak	

33. At the Restaurant / No Restaurante

Dessert	A sobremesa
Beverages	
Coffee	
Tea	
Soda	
Lemonade	
Orange juice	
Alcoholic drinks	
Beer	
Wine	
Check	
Tip	
How may I help you?	
What would you like to order?	
May I have the menu, please?	
Could I get more water, please?	
My order is wrong	
The service here is wonderful!	
The food is delicious!	
The check, please	
The tip is included	

34. The Office
/ A Oficina

Book	O livro
Calculator	
Computer	
Desk	
Fax machine	
File	
File cabinet	
Folder	
Keyboard	
Monitor	
Mouse	
Notebook	
Pad	
Paper	
Pen	
Printer	
Ruler	
Scissors	
Screen	
Stapler	
Telephone	
My computer is broken	
There is no paper in the printer	
We need to buy more folders	
We don't have a copy machine	

35. Jobs and Positions / **Os Trabalhos e os Postos**

Accountant	O contador/A contadora
Architect	
Artist	
Chef	
Clerk	
Cook	
Doctor	
Engineer	
Gardener	
Graphic designer	
Lawyer	
Nurse	
Physician	
Salesperson	
Secretary	
Security guard	
Taxi driver	
Teacher	
Technician	
Tourist guide	
Travel agent	

36. Job Interview / A Entrevista de Trabalho

Apply for a job	Pedir emprego
Duty	
Experience	
Last name	
First name	
Full time job	
Part time job	
Résumé	
Skill	
Work	

37. The Transportation / Os Meios de Transporte

Airplane	O avião
Bicycle	
Bus	
Car	
Helicopter	
Metro	
Motorcycle	
Train	
Truck	

38. The Traffic / O Trânsito

Bus stop	A parada de ônibus
Crosswalk	
Freeway, highway	
Gas station	
Intersection	
Lane	
No outlet	
One way	
Pedestrian	
Speed	
Stop sign	
To get in	
To get off	
Toll	
Traffic light	
Train station	
Two way	
U-turn	
Yield	
I get in the car	
I get off the car	
We wait for the train	

39. The Car
/ O Automóvel

Accelerator	O acelerador
Battery	
Hood	
Brake	
Clutch	
Engine	
Fender	
Gear box	
Headlight	
Rear view mirror	
Make	
Model	
Radiator	
Steering wheel	
Seat	
Tire	
Trunk	
Wheel	
Windshield	
Windshield wipers	
The car is broken	
I have a flat tire	
I need a new battery	
What year is the car?	
What make is the car?	
What model is the car?	
How many miles does the car have?	

40. Phone Conversations / **Conversas Telefônicas**

Call	Ligar
Dial	
Directory	
Directory Assistance	
Extension	
Hold on, please	
I'd like to speak to...	
I'll put you through	
I'll transfer your call	
I'm calling about ...	
Just a minute	
Leave a message	
Let me see...	
Phone	
Phone number	
Ring	
Speak	
Speaking	
Take a message	
Talk	
This is...	
Who's calling?	

41. At the Post Office **/ Nos Correios**

Air mail	Correio aéreo
Counter	
Envelope	
Letter	
Mail	
Parcel	
Postcard	
Postman, mailman	
Stamp	
To send	
To deliver	
Delivery	
To pick up	
Address	
I want to send a letter	
I would like to pick up a parcel	
How much do the stamps cost?	
Do you sell postcards?	

42. At the Bank / No Banco

English	Portuguese
Account	A conta
ATM	
Bank statement	
Bank teller	
Cash	
Checkbook	
Checking account	
Credit card	
Debit card	
Deposit slip	
Savings account	
To deposit	
To save	
To transfer	
To withdraw	
Transactions	
Withdrawal slip	
I want to make a deposit	
Do you have a savings account?	
I have a checking account	
What is your credit card number?	
I don't have an ATM card	
Where are the deposit slips?	

43. At the Airport / No Aeroporto

Arrival	A chegada
Concourse	
Customs	
Departure	
Destination	
Entrance	
Exit	
First class	
Flight	
Gate	
Immigrations office	
Luggage	
Passport	
Restrooms	
Suitcase	
To arrive	
To depart	
To travel	
Trip	
Where are you traveling?	
May I have your ticket, please?	
I need you passport, please	
My flight number is ...	
Where is gate number ...?	
The flight is delayed	
The flight is on time	

44. At the Hotel **/ No Hotel**

Double room	O quarto com duas camas
Single room	
Bell desk	
Bellman	
Elevator	
Reception	
Receptionist	
Reservation	
Stairway	
Swimming pool	
Tours desk	
Valet parking	
To check-in	
To check-out	
I would like to make a reservation	
I want a single room	
I would like to check-in	

45. The Clothes **/ A Roupa**

Bathing suit	A roupa de banho / O biquini
Belt	
Blouse	
Coat	
Dress	
Gloves	
Hat	
Jacket	
Pants	
Purse	
Scarf	
Shirt	
Shoes	
Shorts	
Skirt	
Socks	
Suit	
Suitcase	
The size	
Small	
Medium	
Large	
Big sizes	

46. At the Shopping Center / No Shopping

Department store	Seção, Departamento
Ladies	
Men	
Juniors	
Kids	
Ladies' department	
Jewelry	
Fitting room	
Elevator	
Escalator	
How may I help you?	
I'm looking for ...	
I'm just looking	
Where is the fitting room?	
It fits well	
It doesn't fit well	
May I pay here?	
I want to exchange this	
I want to return this	
I like ...	
I like this blouse	
I don't like ...	
I don't like these pants	

47. At the Drugstore / Na Farmácia

Antiseptic	O desinfetante
Adhesive bandage	
Antibiotic	
Aspirin	
Bandage	
Cold medicine	
Cough syrup	
Medication	
Ointment	
OTC (Over The Counter) medication	
Painkiller	
Pills	
Prescription	
Tablets	
Thermometer	
Cotton	

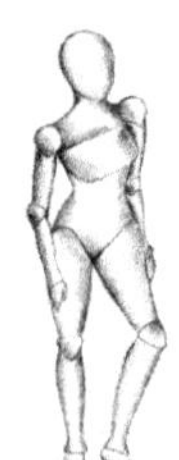

48. The Parts of the Body **/ As parte do Corpo**

Ankle	O tornozelo
Arm	
Back	
Buttock	
Calf	
Chest	
Elbow	
Feet	
Finger	
Foot	
Forearm	
Hand	
Head	
Hip	
Knee	
Leg	
Neck	
Shoulder	
Stomach	
Thigh	
Toe	
Waist	
Wrist	

49. Health Problems / Problemas de Saúde

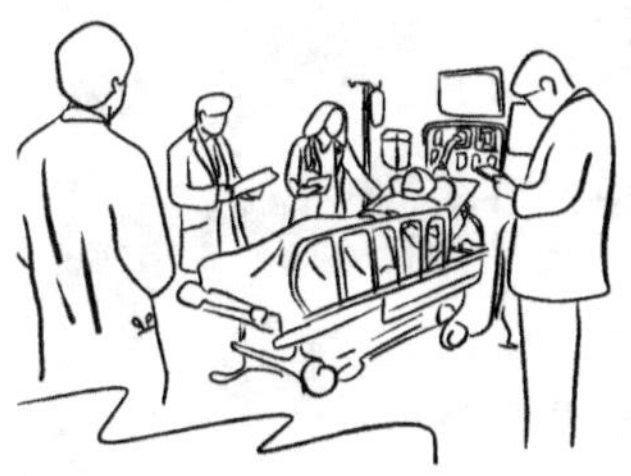

Backache — Dor nas costas

Cold

Fever

Hurt

Indigestion

Injury

Pain

Pulse

Sick

Sneeze

Sore throat

Toothache

I have a headache

I have a stomachache

I have pain in my knee

I hurt my hand

I've got a cold

My foot hurts

50. The Animals **/ Os Animais**

Bear	O urso
Bird	
Cat	
Chicken	
Cow	
Dog	
Duck	
Elephant	
Fish	
Horse	
Lizard	
Lion	
Monkey	
Mouse	
Rat	
Tiger	

EXERCISE!

Write the English translation.

Keep practicing at:

QuickLanguages.com

1. Greetings / Cumprimentos

Olá!	Hi! / Hello!
Bom dia	
Boa tarde	
Boa noite	
Como está você?	
Bem	
Muito bem	
Obrigado(a)	
Muito obrigado(a)	
De nada	
Bem, obrigado(a)	
E você?	
A gente se vê	
Até logo	
Até amanhã	
Adeus	
Tchau	

2. Introductions and Courtesy Expressions / **Apresentações e Expressões de Cortesia**

Qual o seu nome?	What is your name?
Meu nome é...	
Quem é você?	
Sou...	
Quem é ele/ela?	
Ele é.../Ela é...	
Prazer em conhecê-lo/la	
Prazer em conhecê-lo/la também	
É um prazer	
Desculpe	
Por favor	
Um momento, por favor	
Bem-vindo	
Você primeiro	
Pode repetir, por favor?	
Não compreendo	
Compreendo um pouco	
Você poderia falar mais devagar, por favor?	
Você fala espanhol?	
Como se diz hello em espanhol?	
O que significa isso?	
Falo um pouco de espanhol	

3. Ways to Address to a Person / Maneiras de se Dirigir a uma Pessoa

Senhora	Madam / Ma'am
Senhorita	
Sra.,Srta.	
Senhor	
Senhora	
Senhor	
Doutor	

4. The Articles / Os Artigos

O / a / os / as	The
O automóvel	
Os automóveis	
A casa	
As casas	
Um / uma	
Um automóvel	
Uma casa	
Um / uma	
Um elefante	
Uma maçã	
Uns / umas	
Uns automóveis	
Umas casas	

5. The Subject Pronouns **/ Os Pronomes Pessoais de Sujeito**

Eu

Tu / Você (Vc)

Ele

Ela

Isso

Nós

Vocês

Eles / elas

6. The Possessive Adjectives **/ Os Adjetivos Possessivos**

Mim

Tu

Seu (dele)

Sua (dela)

Seu

Nosso/a

De vocês /Vosso (a)

Seus (deles/delas)

Meu carro

Teu livro

Sua televisão

Nossa casa

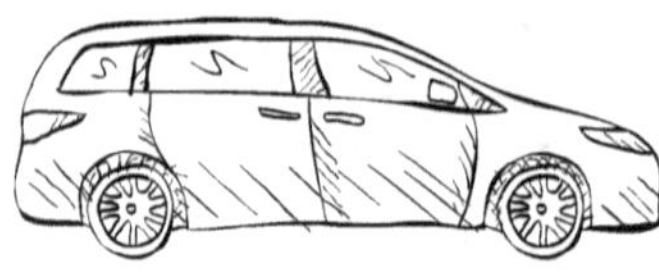

7. The Demonstrative Adjectives / **Os Adjetivos Demonstrativos**

Este / esta	This
Este livro	
Esta camisa	
Estes / estas	
Estes livros	
Estas camisas	
Esse / essa	
Essa mesa	
Esse carro	
Esses / essas	
Essas mesas	
Esses carros	

8. The Possessive Pronouns / **Os Pronomes Possessivos**

Meu	Mine
Teu	
Seu (dele)	
sua (dela)	
Seu	
Nosso/a	
Vosso	
Seu (deles / delas)	
O carro é meu	
O livro é teu	
Essa tevisão é sua	
Esta casa é nossa	

9. The Cardinal Numbers / **Os Numerais Cardinais**

Zero 0 / Zero

Um

Dois

Três

Quatro

Cinco

Seis

Sete

Oito

Nove

Dez

Onze

Doze

Treze

Catorze

Quinze

Dezesseis

Dezessete

dezoito

dezenove

Vinte

Vinte e um

Trinta

Quarenta

Cinquenta

Sessenta

1. 2. 3. 4.
5. 6. 7. 8.
9. 0.

9. The Cardinal Numbers / Os Numerais Cardinais

Setenta 70 / Seventy
Oitenta
Noventa
Cem
Cento e um
Duzentos
Trezentos
Quatrocentos
Quinhentos
Seiscentos
Setecentos
Oitocentos
Novecentos
Mil
Dez mil
Cem mil
Um milhão
Mil milhões
Quarente e cinco
Cento e vinte e oito
Mil novecentos e sessenta e três
Seis mil e trinta e sete
Onze mil
Duzentos e setenta e nove mil
Dois milhões

10. The Time / A Hora

O relógio (de pared)	The clock
O relógio (de pulso)	
Que horas são?	
São...	
É uma hora	
São duas horas	
São três e quinze	
São quatro e trinta / São as quatro e meia	
São cinco e quarenta e cinco / São quinze para as seis	
São seis e cinquenta / São dez para as sete	
É meio-dia	
É meia-noite	
Na manhã	
Na tarde	
Na noite	
Na noite	
Que hora é....?	
Que hora é o show?	
à / às	
Às sete da noite	

11. The Days of the Week / Os Dias da Semana

Segunda-feira	Monday
Terça-feira	
Quarta-feira	
Quinta-feira	
Sexta-feira	
Sábado	
Domingo	
Que dia é hoje?	

12. The Months of the Year / Os Meses do Ano

Janeiro	January
Fevereiro	
Março	
Abril	
Maio	
Junho	
Julho	
Agosto	
Setembro	
Outubro	
Novembro	
Dezembro	
Qual a data de hoje?	

13. The Weather **/ O Clima**

Ensolarado	Sunny
Nublado	
Chuvoso	
Húmido	
Seco	
Frio	
Calor	
Calor	
A chuva	
A neve	
Como está o clima hoje?	
O clima está bom	
Está soleado	
Faz frio no inverno	
Está chovendo	
Está nevando	
Tenho frio	

14. The Seasons **/ As Estações**

Primavera	Spring
Verão	
Outono	
Inverno	

15. The Colors **/ As Cores**

Amarelo	Yellow
Vermelho	
Azul	
Verde	
Laranja	
Marrom	
Cor-de rosa	
Púrpura	
Preto	
Branco	
Cinza	
Claro	
Escuro	
Verde-claro	
Livro laranja	
Sapatos marrons	
Minha blusa é branca	
De que cor é...?	
Qual a tua cor favorita?	

16. The Parts of the Face / As Partes da Casa

A bochecha	Cheek
O queixo	
A orelha	
O olho	
A testa	
O cabelo	
Os lábios	
A boca	
O nariz	
A pele	
Os dentes	
O dente	
Louro / Loura	
Castanho	
Com cabelo branco	
Ruivo	
Comprido	
Curto	
Liso	
Enrrolado	
John é louro	
Karen tem cabelo comprido	
Ele tem olhos verdes	
Seus olhos são azuis	
Seus olhos são grandes e marrons	

17. Essential Verbs **/ Verbos Essenciais**

Português	English
Ser / Estar	Be
Ir	
Vir	
Ter	
Conseguir	
Ajudar	
Amar	
Gostar	
Querer	
Comprar	
Vender	
Ler	
Escrever	
Beber	
Comer	
Abrir	
Fechar	
Olhar	
Buscar	
Encontrar	
Começar	
Parar	
Puxar	

17. Essential Verbs **/ Verbos Essenciais**

Empurrar	Push
Enviar	
Receber	
Acender	
Apagar	
Escutar	
Falar	
Fazer	
Dirigir	
Sentir	
Saber	
Deixar, Sair	
Viver	
Fazer, preparar	
Conhecer, Encontrar-se com	
Necessitar	
Pagar	
Brincar / Jogar	
Lembrar	
Repertir	
Dizer	
Sentar-se	
Dormir	

17. Essential Verbs / Verbos Essenciais

Estudar	Study
Tomar	
Pensar	
Compreender	
Esperar	
Olhar, Observar	
Há	
Há	
(Eu) sou alto	
(Você) é pequeño	
Ele é magro	
(Nós) somos grandes	
(Eles/as) são inteligentes	
(Eu) estou em casa	
(Você) está na escola	
(Nós) estamos na loja	
(Eu) obtenho um prêmio	
(Eu) vou ao cinema	
(Eu) tenho um bonito carro	
(Eu) escuto música	
(Eu) vejo a televisão	
Gosto deste livro	
Há dez crianças no parque	

18. Interrogative Words / Palavras Interrogativas

Quantos/as...?	How many ...?
Quanto/a...?	
Como...?	
Que...?	
Quando...?	
Onde...?	
Qual...?	
Quem...?	
De quem...?	
A quem...?	
Por que?	
Porque?	

19. Linking Words / Conectores

E	And
Mas	
Ou	
Ou...Ou	
Nem...Nem	
Sim	
Não	
Então	
Enquanto	

20. The Prepositions / As Preposições

Sobre	About
Em cima de	
Em frente de, ao largo	
A, em	
Detrás de	
Debaixo de	
Entre	
De (meios de transporte), por	
Abaixo	
Durante	
Por, para	
De, desde	
Em, dentro de	
Em frente de / diante de	
Dentro	

20. The Prepositions / As Preposições

Perto	Near
Junto de	
De	
Em, sobre	
Fora	
Sobre, por em cima	
Por	
Através	
Para(para alguém), até	
Debaixo	
Em cima	
Com	
Sem	
O gato está dentro da caixa	
O vaso de flores está sobre a mesa	
Alguém está na porta	

21. Giving Directions / **Dando instruções para chegar a um lugar**

Na esquina	At the corner
Longe	
Perto	
Continue tudo direto	
Esquerda	
Direita	
Dobre à esquerda	
Dobre à direita	
Continue direto um bloco mais	
Depois do semáforo, dobre à direita	
Como posso chegar a...?	
Onde está o / a...?	
Onde fica a Igreja?	
O museu está do lado do shopping	
A farmácia está em frente do edificio	
O supermercado está perto do parque	

22. The Ordinal Numbers **/ Os Numerais Ordinais**

Portuguese	English
Primeiro	First
Segundo	
Terceiro	
Quarto	
Quinto	
Sexto	
Sétimo	
Oitavo	
Nono	
Décimo	
Décimo primeiro	
Décimo segundo	
Vigésimo	
Trigésimo	
O primeiro edificio	
O segundo andar	

23. Countries, Nationalities, and Languages / **Paises, Nacionalidades e Idiomas**

Brasil (País)	Brazil (Country)
brasileiro/a (nacionalidade)	
Português (idioma)	
Colômbia	
colombiano/a	
espanhol	
China	
Chinês/chinesa	
Chinês	
Inglaterra	
inglês/a	
inglês	
França	
francês/a	
francês	
Alemanha	
alemão/alemã	
alemão	
Itália	

23. Countries, Nationalities, and Languages / **Paises, Nacionalidades e Idiomas**

Portuguese	English
Italiano/a	Italian
Italiano/a	
Japão	
japonês/a	
japonês	
México	
mexicano/a	
espanhol	
Espanha	
espanhol/a	
espanhol	
Estados Unidos de América	
americano/a	
inglês	
De onde você é?	
Eu sou do Brasil	
Eu sou brasileiro	
Eu falo português	
Eu não sou da Itália	

24. Indefinite Pronouns / Pronomes Indefinidos

Alguém (interrogativo), ninguém (negativo)	Anybody
Alguma coisa (interrogativo), nada (negativo)	
Ninguém	
Nada	
Alguém (afirmativo)	
Alguma coisa (afirmativo)	
Todos	
Tudo	
Tem alguém em casa?	
Não quero nada	
Não aconteceu nada	
Alguém está na sala	
Tudo está pronto	

25. The Emotions / As Emoções

Com raiva, chateado	Angry
Entediado	
Seguro de si mesmo	
Confuso	
Envergonhado	
Entusiasmado	
Contente	
Nervoso	
Orgulhoso	
Triste	
Assustado	
Tímido	
Surpreendido	
Preocupado	
(Eu)estou contente	
Ele está triste	
Eles estão surpreendidos	
Você está entusiasmada?	
(Eu)não estou entediado	
Ela não está nervosa	
Todos estão seguros de si mesmos	

26. Adverbs / Advérbios

Uns poucos — A few

Um pouco

Muito

Depois

Outra vez

Atrás

Também

Sempre

Antes

Suficientemente

Todos os dias

exatamente

Finalmente

Em primeiro lugar

aquí

Tarde

Mais tarde

Nunca

Próximo

Agora

26. Adverbs **/ Advérbios**

Freqüentemente	often
Uma vez	
Somente	
Fora	
Realmente	
Aquí mesmo	
Agora mesmo	
Desde	
Lentamente	
Às vezes	
Em breve	
Ainda	
Logo	
Lá	
Hoje	
Amanhã	
Esta noite	
Também	
Geralmente	

27. Auxiliary Verbs / Verbos Auxiliares

Português	English
Poder (para habilidades e pedidos informais)	Can
Poder (para pedidos formais)	
∅	
Fazer (auxiliar para o presente simples)	
Fazer (auxiliar para o presente simples - terceira pessoa)	
Ter que	
Poder (para pedir licença)	
Dever (obrigação)	
Dever (para dar conselhos)	
∅	
∅	
Você pode ir ao cinema?	
Você poderia me dar dinheiro trocado?	
Trabalhaste na farmácia?	
(Eu) trabalhei na farmácia	
Trabalhas na farmácia?	
(Eu) não trabalho na farmácia	
Ele lê o jornal?	
Ele não lê o jornal	
(Eu) tenho que fazer a minha tarefa.	
Posso lhe ajudar?	
(Você) deve dobrar à esquerda agora	
(Você) deveria ir ao doutor	
(Eu) trabalharei amanhã	
(Eu) gostaria de uma taça de vinho	

28. Expressions / Espressões

Está bem — All right

Entre

Venha por aquí, por favor

Não te preocupes!

Por exemplo

Boa sorte!

Exelente idéia!

Que tenha um bom dia!

Sírva-se alguma coisa!

Aquí tens

Mais depressa

Concordo

Não concordo

Não me importo

Não sei

Já vou

Tenho medo de que...

Trato feito!

Que você continue estando bem!

Deixe-me pensar

Vamos!

Neste momento

Soa bem

Com certeza

Sente-se

Cuide-se!

29. The Family / A Família

O pai	Father
A mãe	
O filho	
A filha	
O irmão	
A irmã	
O avô	
A avó	
O tio	
A tia	
O primo/a	
O sobrinho	
A sobrinha	
O esposo	
A esposa	
O namorado	
A namorada	
Os parentes políticos	
O sogro	
A sogra	
O cunhado	
A cunhada	
O padrasto	
A madrasta	
O irmão de criação	
A irmã de criação	
Quem é ele?	
Ele é meu irmão	

30. The House / A casa

A sala — Living room

A porta

A janela

O sofá

A lâmpada

sala de jantar

A mesa

A cadeira

A cozinha

O aquecedor

O forno

A geladeira

O microonda

O quarto

A cama

A mesa de cabeceira

Cómoda com espelho

A cómoda

O guarda-roupa

O banheiro

O espelho

A pia

O sanitário

A bacia

A lavanderia

O estacionamento

Onde está a sala?

A porta é grande

O aquecedor é pequeño

A cozinha é bonita

31. The City / **A Cidade**

O bloco	Block
O edificio	
A igreja	
O cinema	
O museu	
O parque	
A farmácia	
O restaurante	
O shopping	
A loja	
A rua	
O supermercado	

32. At the Supermarket **/ No Supermercado**

Os alimentos	The food
As frutas	
A maçã	
A banana	
A cereja	
As uvas	
A laranja	
O morango	
Os vegetais	
Os feijões	
A cenoura	
O couve-flor	
O alface	
Cebola	
O pimentão	
A batata	
O tomate	
As carnes	
A carne de vaca	
A carne de frango	
O perú	
O presunto	
A carne de porco	
Os produtos lácteos	
A manteiga	
O queijo	
O leite	

32. At the Supermarket / No Supermercado

Portuguese	English
O iogurte	Yogurt
A geléia	
O pão	
Os ovos	
O peixe	
Os mariscos	
A lata	
O carrinho	
A bolsa	
A cesta	
A garrafa	
A caixa registradora	
Ele / ela caixa	
Serviço ao cliente	
As compras	
Quantos/as...?	
Quantas laranjas você compra?	
Quanto custa...?	
Quanto custam as bananas?	
Eu quero...	
Eu quero comprar uma garrafa de leite	
Eu gostaria.../queria...	
Eu queria uma bolsa de tomates	
Onde está o alface?	
Está na seção um	
Onde estão as latas dos vegetais?	
Estão na seção cinco	

33. At the Restaurant **/ No Restaurante**

O garçom/a garçonete	Waiter / waitress
Café-da manhã	
Almoço	
Janta	
Comer	
Beber	
Tomar o café-da manhã	
A carta	
O aperitivo	
A salada	
A sopa	
O prato principal	
As massas	
O arroz	
As batatas fritas	
O purê de batatas	
As batatas ao forno	
O churrasco	
O frango frito	
A bisteca	

33. At the Restaurant / No Restaurante

A sobremesa	Dessert
As bebidas	
O café	
O chá	
A bebida com gás	
A limonada	
O suco de laranja	
As bebidas alcoólicas	
A cerveja	
O vinho	
A conta	
A gorjeta	
Como posso lhe ajudar?	
O que você deseja?	
Você pode me dar o menu, por favor?	
Você poderia me trazer mais água, por favor?	
Esta não é a minha ordem	
O serviço daquí é exelente!	
A comida está deliciosa!	
A conta, por favor	
A gorgeta está incluida	

34. The Office
/ A Oficina

Portuguese	English
O livro	Book
A calculadora	
O computador	
Mesa de oficina	
A máquina de fax	
O expediente	
O arquivador	
A pasta	
O techado	
O monitor	
O mouse	
O caderno	
O bloco	
O papel	
A caneta	
A impressora	
A régua	
A tesoura	
A tela	
O grampeador	
O telefone	
Meu computador está rebentado	
Não tem papel na impressora	
Precisamos comprar mais pastas	
Não temos fotocopiadora	

35. Jobs and Positions / **Os Trabalhos e os Postos**

O contador/A contadora	Accountant
O arquiteto	
O artista	
O chef de cozinha	
O empregado/A empregada	
O cozinheiro/ A cozinheira	
O doutor/ A doutora	
O engenheiro	
O jardineiro	
O designer gráfico/ A designer gráfico	
O advogado	
O enfermeiro/ A enfermeira	
O médico	
O vendedor/ A vendedora	
A secretária	
O guarda de segurança	
O taxista	
O professor/ A professora	
O técnico	
O guia turístico	
O agente de viagens	

36. Job Interview
/ A Entrevista de Trabalho

Pedir emprego	Apply for a job
Tarefa	
Esxperiência	
Sobrenome	
Nome	
Trabalho em tempo integral	
Trabalho de meia jornada	
Currículum vitae	
Habilidade	
Trabalhar / O trabalho	

37. The Transportation
/ Os Meios de Transporte

O avião	Airplane
A bicicleta	
O ônibus	
O automóvel	
O helicóptero	
O metrô	
A moto	
O trem	
O caminhão	

38. The Traffic / O Trânsito

A parada de ônibus	Bus stop
A faixa para pedestres	
A rodovia	
O posto de gasolina	
O cruzamento de ruas	
A faixa (de uma rodovia)	
O caminho sem saída	
Um só sentido	
O pedestre	
A velocidade	
O sinal de stop	
Subir, entrar	
Descer, sair	
O pedágio	
O semáforo	
A estação ferroviária	
Duas vias	
Girar em U	
Dar passo	
(Eu) subo no carro	
(Eu) desço do carro	
(Nós) esperamos o trem	

39. The Car
/ O Automóvel

O acelerador	Accelerator
A bateria	
O capô	
O freio	
A embreagem	
O motor	
O pára-choques	
A caixa de velocidades	
A luz	
O espelho retrovisor	
A marca	
O modelo	
O radiador	
O volante	
O assento	
O pneu	
O porta-mala	
A roda	
O pára-brisas	
O limpa pára-brisas	
O carro está quebrado	
Desinchou um pneu	
Preciso de uma bateria nova	
De que ano é o carro?	
Qual a marca do carro?	
Qual o modelo do carro?	
Quantos kilômetros tem o carro?	

40. Phone Conversations / **Conversas Telefônicas**

Ligar	Call
Discar	
A guia telefônica	
A informação	
O número interno	
Não desligue, por favor/ Um momento, por favor	
Queria falar com...	
Lhe comunicarei	
Transferirei sua ligação	
Ligo por...	
Espere um minuto	
Deixar uma mensagem	
Deixe-me ver	
Telefone/ Ligar	
Número de telefone	
Soar	
Falar	
Fala ele/ela	
escrever uma mensagem	
Falar	
Sou / Fala...	
Quem é / Quem fala	

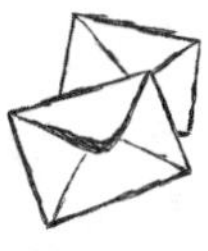

41. At the Post Office / Nos Correios

Correio aéreo	Air mail
O balcão	
O envelope	
A carta	
A correspondência	
O pacote	
O cartão postal	
O carteiro	
O selo	
Enviar	
Entregar	
A entrega	
retirar	
O endereço	
Quero enviar uma carta	
Gostaris de retirar um pacote	
Quanto custam os selos?	
Vocês vendem cartões postais?	

42. At the Bank / **No Banco**

Portuguese	English
A conta	Account
A caixa eletrônica	
O resume bancário	
O / A caixa	
O dinheiro	
O talão de cheques	
A conta corrente	
O cartão de crédito	
O cartão de débito	
O comprovante de depósito	
A caderneta de poupança	
Depositar	
Poupar	
Transferir	
Retirar	
As transações	
O comprovante de retiro	
Quero fazer um depósito	
Você tem uma conta poupança?	
Tenho uma conta corrente	
Qual o número do seu cartão de crédito?	
Não tenho cartão do caixa eletrônico	
Onde estão os comprovantes de depósito?	

43. At the Airport / No Aeroporto

A chegada Arrival

O corredor

A alfândega

A partida

O destino

A entrada

A saída

Primeira classe

O vôo

A porta

A oficina de Imigrações

A equipagem

O passaporte

Os banheiros

A mala

Chegar

Partir

Viajar

A viagem

Para onde você vai viajar?

Pode me dar a sua passagem?

Preciso do seu passaporte, por favor

Meu número de vôo é...

Onde está a porta de número...

O vôo está atrasado

O vôo está a tempo

44. At the Hotel **/ No Hotel**

O quarto com duas camas	Double room
O quarto com uma cama	
O porteiro	
O auxiliar de serviços	
O elevador	
A recepção	
O / A recepcionista	
A reserva	
As escadas	
A piscina	
O posto de turismo	
O serviço de estacionamento	
Registrar-se	
Pagar a conta do hotel	
Gostaria de fazer uma reserva	
Quero um quarto com uma cama	
Eu gostaria de me registrar	

45. The Clothes
/ A Roupa

A roupa de banho / O biquini Bathing suit

O cinto

A blusa

O casaco

O vestido

As luvas

O chapéu

A jaqueta

As calças

A carteira

O cachecol

A camisa

Os sapatos

Os shorts

A saia

As meias

O terno

A mala

O tamanho

Pequeño

Médio

Grande

Tamanhos grandes

46. At the Shopping Center / No Shopping

Seção, Departamento	Department store
Senhoras	
Senhores	
Jovens	
Crianças	
Seção de senhoras	
Joalheria	
Provador	
Elevador	
Escada mecânica	
Como posso lhe ajudar?	
Estou buscando...	
Só estou olhando	
Onde está o provador?	
Fica bem em mim	
Não fica muito bem em mim	
Posso pagar aquí?	
Quero mudar esto	
Quero devolver esto	
Eu gosto...	
Gosto desta blusa	
Eu não gosto...	
Eu não gosto desta calça	

47. At the Drugstore **/ Na Farmácia**

O desinfetante	Antiseptic
O band-aid	
O antibiótico	
A aspirina	
O curativo	
O remédio para o resfriado	
O xarope para a tosse	
Os remédios	
A pomada	
Os remédios sem receita	
O calmante	
Os comprimidos	
A receita médica	
As tabelas	
O termômetro	
O algodão	

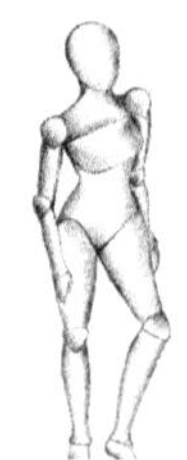

48. The Parts of the Body **/ As parte do Corpo**

O tornozelo	Ankle
O braço	
As costas	
A bunda	
Panturrilha	
O peito	
O cotovelo	
Os pés	
O dedo da mão	
O pé	
Antebraço	
A mão	
A cabeça	
O quadril	
O joelho	
A perna	
O pescoço	
O ombro	
O estômago	
A coxa	
O dedo do pé	
A cintura	
O pulso	

49. Health Problems / Problemas de Saúde

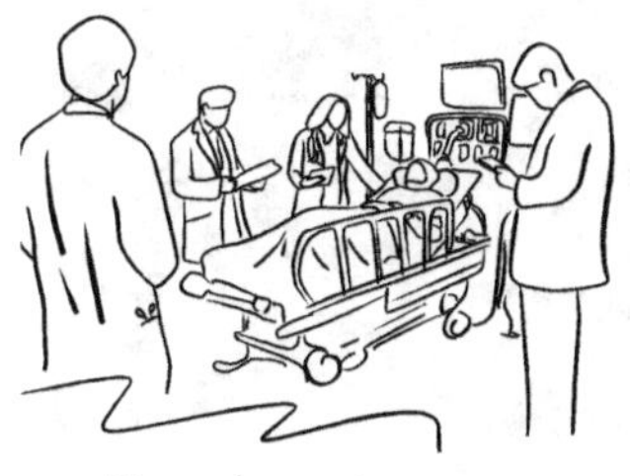

Dor nas costas	Backache
O resfriado	
A febre	
Ferir-se, magoar-se, machucar-se	
A indigestão	
A ferida	
A dor	
O pulso	
Doente	
O espirro	
A dor de garganta	
A dor de dente	
Tenho dor de cabeça	
Tenho dor de estômago	
Dói o meu joelho	
Machuquei a minha mão	
Tenho um resfriado	
Dói o meu pé	

50. The Animals / Os Animais

O urso	Bear
O pássaro	
O gato	
O frango	
A vaca	
O cachorro	
O pato	
O elefante	
O peixe	
O cavalo	
A lagartixa	
O leão	
O macaco	
O rato	
O rato	
O tigre	

QUICK LANGUAGES

MULTI-LANGUAGE PHRASEBOOK COLLECTION

SPEAK ANY LANGUAGE NOW!

QUICK LANGUAGES PHRASEBOOK COLLECTION AVAILABLE TITLES

1. ENGLISH-SPANISH & SPANISH-ENGLISH
2. ENGLISH-ITALIAN & ITALIAN-ENGLISH
3. ENGLISH-FRENCH & FRENCH-ENGLISH
4. ENGLISH-GERMAN & GERMAN-ENGLISH
5. ENGLISH-PORTUGUESE & PORTUGUESE-ENGLISH
6. ENGLISH-CHINESE & CHINESE-ENGLISH
7. ENGLISH-ARABIC & ARABIC-ENGLISH
8. ENGLISH-JAPANESE & JAPANESE-ENGLISH
9. ENGLISH-KOREAN & KOREAN-ENGLISH
10. ENGLISH-RUSSIAN & RUSSIAN-ENGLISH
11. ENGLISH-TURKISH & TURKISH-ENGLISH

www.ingramcontent.com/pod-product-compliance
Lightning Source LLC
LaVergne TN
LVHW050648100826
845148LV00011B/2035

* 9 7 8 1 6 8 1 6 5 6 1 1 3 *